guitar

chords

... a handy beginner's guide!

D1298858

Published by **Wise Publications**

Exclusive Distributors: Music Sales Limited,
14-15 Berners Street, London W1T 3LJ, UK

Order No. AM1008381
ISBN 978-1-78305-453-4

Edited by Ruth Power.
Inside layout by Fresh Lemon.

Made in China.

www.musicsales.com

Contents

Reading chord diagrams

Each chord in this book is displayed in three ways:

1. With a chord diagram to show left-hand fingering
2. In standard notation to show the notes of the chord
3. In a photograph to show the left-hand position

Chord diagrams

Chord diagrams show the guitar neck face-on. Finger positions are indicated as illustrated:

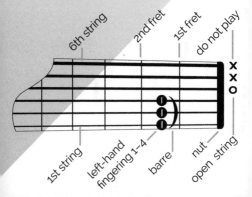

6th string

2nd fret

1st fret

do not play

1st string

left-hand fingering 1–4

barre

nut

open string

OPEN CHORDS

A

A C♯ E

9

A

OPEN CHORDS

A7   A C♯ E G

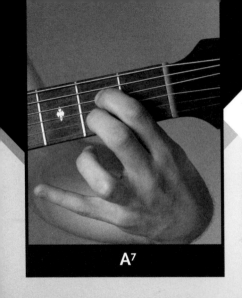

A⁷

Am

OPEN CHORDS
Am⁷
A C E G

Am⁷

OPEN CHORDS

B⁷

B D♯ F♯ A

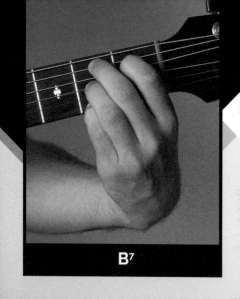

B⁷

OPEN CHORDS

C

C E G

C

OPEN CHORDS
Cadd⁹
C E G D

Cadd⁹

OPEN CHORDS

Cmaj7

C E G B

Cmaj⁷

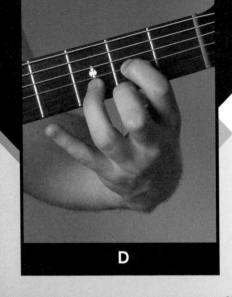

D

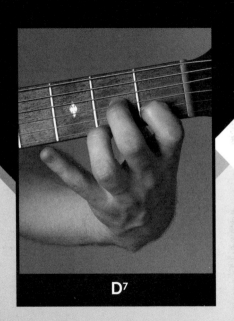

D⁷

OPEN CHORDS
Dm
D F A

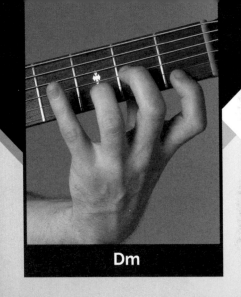

Dm

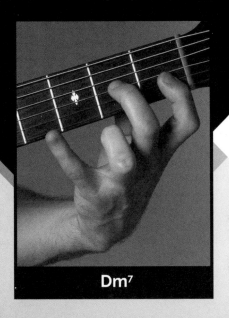

Dm⁷

OPEN CHORDS
Dmaj⁷

D F♯ A C♯

Dmaj⁷

Dsus⁴

OPEN CHORDS

E

E G♯ B

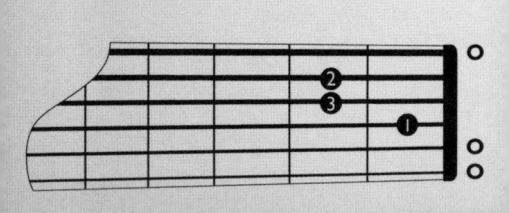

E

35

OPEN CHORDS
E⁷
E G♯ B D

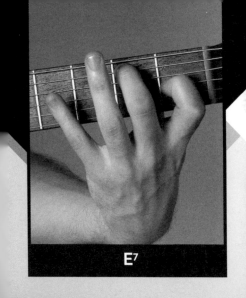

E⁷

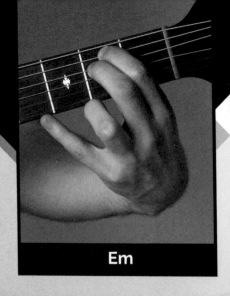

Em

Em⁷

41

F

43

OPEN CHORDS
Fmaj7
F A C E

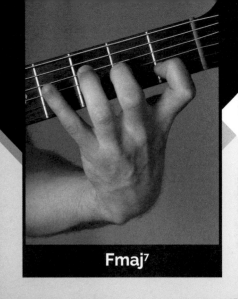

Fmaj⁷

OPEN CHORDS

G

G B D

G

G⁷

G B D F

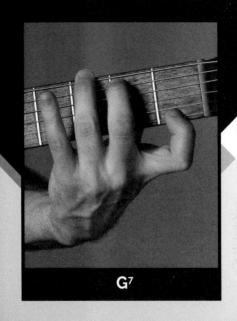

G⁷

Barre Chords

Barre chords are special chord shapes which can be moved up and down the guitar neck.

The 'barre' is formed by fretting across five or six strings with the first finger. The remaining three fingers fret the other notes of the chord.

Here you will learn E-shape barre chords (with their root on the 6th string) and A-shape barre chords (with their root on the 5th string).

Up the fretboard

Barre chords allow you to play different chords by moving one hand position up the guitar neck.

In this example, an A shape major barre chord played at the 2nd fret is a B chord; the same shape moved up to the 3rd fret is a C chord.

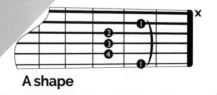

A shape

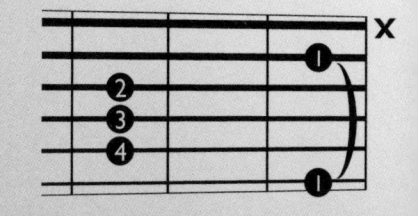

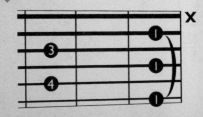

BARRE CHORDS
Am shape

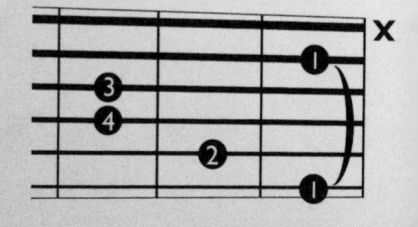

A shape Barre Chord

Am shape Barre Chord

BARRE CHORDS
E shape

BARRE CHORDS
E⁷ shape

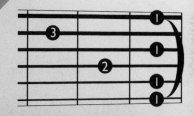

59

BARRE CHORDS
Em shape

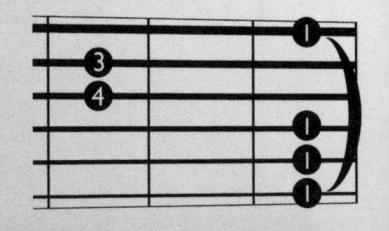

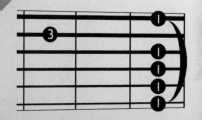

E shape Barre Chord

Em shape Barre Chord

Power Chords

A '**power chord**' is made up of the root note and the fifth note in the chord scale. It is also referred to as a 'five chord' and looks like this; A^5. This chord has no major or minor quality since it doesn't have a third.

Power chords are often used in rock music on the electric guitar because they sound great with distortion. They are also easier to play at a fast pace because they all use one basic shape, simply moved around different frets.

Power chord shape

POWER CHORDS

A⁵

A E

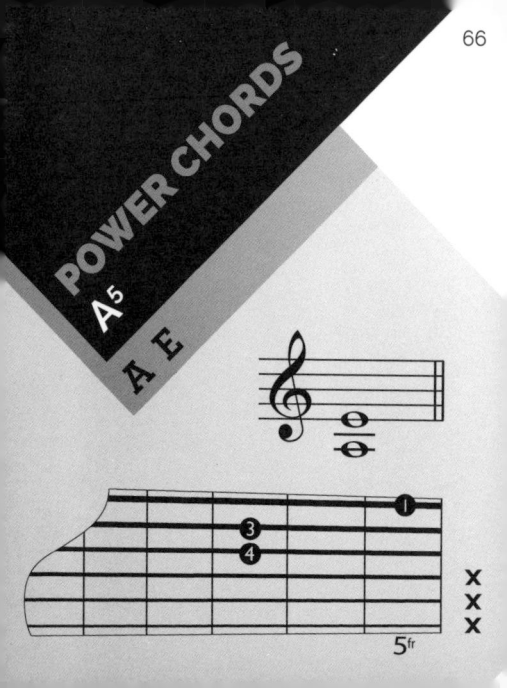

5fr

POWER CHORDS

B♭5

B♭ F

6fr

x x x

POWER CHORDS

B5 F#

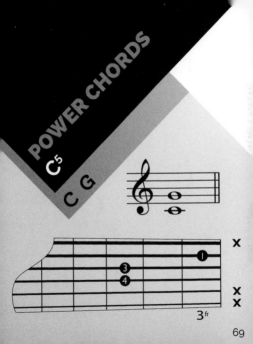

POWER CHORDS

C5

C G

3fr

X

XX

69

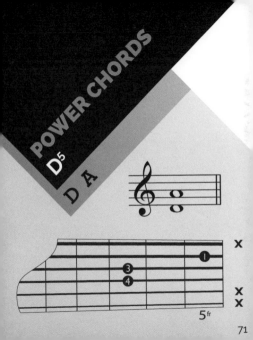

POWER CHORDS

D⁵

D A

5 fr

POWER CHORDS

E♭5

E♭ B♭

6fr

POWER CHORDS

E⁵

E B

7 fr

73

POWER CHORDS

F⁵

F C

x x x

POWER CHORDS

F#5

F# C#

75

A♭5

A♭ E♭

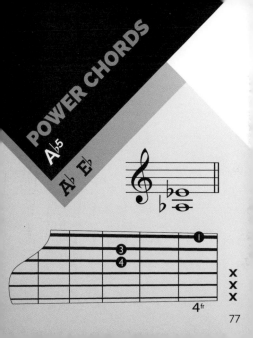

X X X

4fr

What you've learnt:

You've learned how to read chord diagrams and learned to play and recognise three main types of chords:

- Open chord
- Barre chords
- Power chords

With these chords you will be able to play hundreds of songs. Most pop, rock and blues songs will use chords covered in this flipbook. But there are many more chords you can learn to deepen your knowledge of guitar playing.

MORE IN THE Playbook SERIES

available from all good music shops
or in case of difficulty contact: music@musicsales.co.uk

Listen to jazz musicians or skilled metal players and you'll notice some of the chords they use are much more complex in their harmony. You can learn these chords too! It just takes practice and patience.

Once you can play the chords in this flipbook easily, you can then move on to some of the more complex chords which you will find in the recommended books on the next page. Good luck!